UNDERSTANDING WEATHER

Cloud Cover

by Kristin Schuetz

Adams 12 Five Star Schools
1500 E 128th Avenue
Thornton, CO 80241
(720) 972-4000

BLASTOFF! READERS
2

BELLWETHER MEDIA · MINNEAPOLIS, MN

Note to Librarians, Teachers, and Parents:

Blastoff! Readers are carefully developed by literacy experts and combine standards-based content with developmentally appropriate text.

Level 1 provides the most support through repetition of high-frequency words, light text, predictable sentence patterns, and strong visual support.

Level 2 offers early readers a bit more challenge through varied simple sentences, increased text load, and less repetition of high-frequency words.

Level 3 advances early-fluent readers toward fluency through increased text and concept load, less reliance on visuals, longer sentences, and more literary language.

Level 4 builds reading stamina by providing more text per page, increased use of punctuation, greater variation in sentence patterns, and increasingly challenging vocabulary.

Level 5 encourages children to move from "learning to read" to "reading to learn" by providing even more text, varied writing styles, and less familiar topics.

Whichever book is right for your reader, Blastoff! Readers are the perfect books to build confidence and encourage a love of reading that will last a lifetime!

This edition first published in 2016 by Bellwether Media, Inc.
No part of this publication may be reproduced in whole or in part without written permission of the publisher.
For information regarding permission, write to Bellwether Media, Inc., Attention: Permissions Department, 6012 Blue Circle Dr., Minnetonka, MN 55343.

Library of Congress Cataloging-in-Publication Data
Schuetz, Kristin.
  Cloud Cover / by Kristin Schuetz.
    pages cm – (Blastoff! Readers: Understanding Weather)
  Summary: "Relevant images match informative text in this introduction to cloud cover. Intended for students kindergarten through third grade"–Provided by publisher.
  Audience: Ages 5-8
  Audience: K to grade 3
  Includes bibliographical references and index.
  ISBN: 978-1-62617-250-0 (hardcover : alk. paper)
  ISBN: 978-1-62617-504-4 (paperback : alk. paper)
  1. Clouds–Juvenile literature. 2. Fog–Juvenile literature. I. Title.
  QC921.35.S38 2016
  551.57'6–dc23
                                                    2015004209

Table of Contents

Forecasting With Clouds

The clouds in the sky tell a lot about the weather.

Thick clumps of clouds can block the sun's warmth. Gray and green clouds can mean storms.

Meteorologists talk about cloud cover in their **forecasts**.

FIRST ALERT WEATHER 5 — SATURDAY

45°

DAYBREAK

► MOSTLY CLOUDY
► DRY
► LIGHT WINDS

WINDS: E 5-10 SUNRISE: 7:34 AM

MOSTLY CLOUDY

THUR

HIGH
63

LOW
43

They **predict** how much open sky will show. They warn if rain clouds are coming.

Types of Cloud Cover

Sometimes the sky is bright blue with very few clouds.

This kind of cloud cover is called **clear**.

Other times, only patches of sunny, blue sky show. Clouds cover up as much as half of the sky.

This cover is called **scattered**.

Even more clouds fill a **broken** sky.

This sky is also called mostly
cloudy. Little sunlight can
peek through.

An **overcast** sky is fully covered by clouds. Sunlight cannot break through.

If the clouds are dark, they might be thick with **precipitation**.

Low Visibility

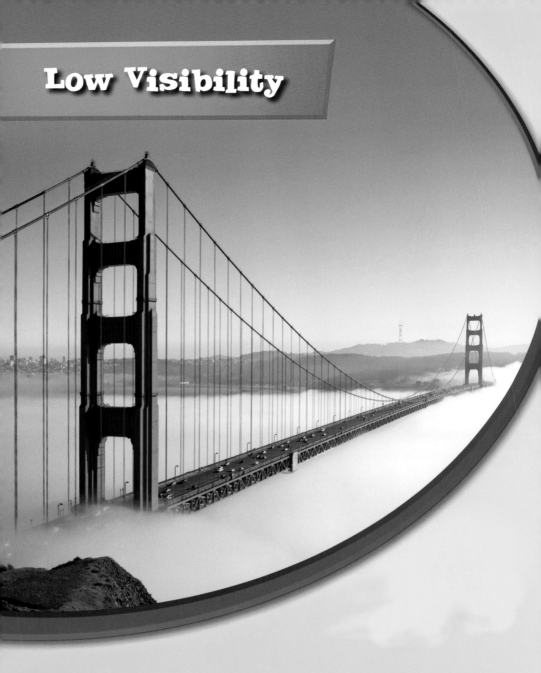

Sometimes **fog**, snow, or dust can **obscure** the sky.

Then the cloud cover is difficult to see. This is called low **visibility**.

Effects of Cloud Cover

A cloudy sky can keep daytime **temperatures** cool. Clouds **shield** the earth from the hot sun.

At night, clouds keep
temperatures warmer.
They trap heat close
to the earth.

Clouds do not protect us from the sun's harmful rays.

Those rays can still pass through clouds. Watch out for **sunburn**!

Glossary

broken—when more than half of the sky is filled with clouds

clear—when the sky has few or no clouds

fog—a cloud that is low to the ground

forecasts—guesses about what the weather will be like

meteorologists—people who study and predict the weather

obscure—to hide or make hard to see

overcast—when most or all of the sky is filled with clouds

precipitation—water that falls from the sky as rain, hail, or snow

predict—to tell ahead of time what might happen

scattered—when up to half of the sky is filled with clouds

shield—to protect by blocking

sunburn—burned and blistered skin; being out in the sun for too long without sunscreen or other protection causes sunburn.

temperatures—measures of how hot or cold it is outside

visibility—the ability to see something clearly

To Learn More

AT THE LIBRARY

Cox Cannons, Helen. *Clouds.* Chicago, Ill.: Heinemann Library, 2015.

Delano, Marfe Ferguson. *Clouds.* Washington, D.C.: National Geographic, 2015.

Hall, Katharine. *Clouds: A Compare and Contrast Book.* Mount Pleasant, S.C.: Arbordale Publishing, 2014.

ON THE WEB

Learning more about cloud cover is as easy as 1, 2, 3.

1. Go to www.factsurfer.com.

2. Enter "cloud cover" into the search box.

3. Click the "Surf" button and you will see a list of related web sites.

With factsurfer.com, finding more information is just a click away.

Index

The images in this book are reproduced through the courtesy of: emmgunn, front cover; Pakhnyushchy, front cover, pp. 8-9 (background); solarseven, weather symbols (front cover, all interior pages); photo.ua, pp. 4-5, 6 (background); irin-k, pp. 4-5 (background); michaeljung, p. 6; Masterfile/ Corbis, pp. 8-9; Marius Szczygiel, p. 10; Sergey Novikov, p. 11; Yuriy Kulik, pp. 12-13; Beau Lark/ Corbis, p. 14; stocker1970, pp. 14-15; Manamana, p. 16; CEFutcher, p. 17; Yva Momatiuk & John Eastcott/ Corbis, pp. 18-19; Steve Elms/ Corbis, p. 19; Jim David, p. 20; karelnoppe, p. 21.